# THE DATING DUPLEX

## Learn The Secrets To Start Dating The Right Way

## Lawrence Burke

# Table of Contents

# Chapter 1:

## _6 Ways To Attract Anything You Want In Life_

It is common human nature that one wants whatever one desires in life. People work their ways to get what they need or want. This manifestation of wanting to attract things is almost in every person around us. A human should be determined to work towards his goal or dreams through sheer hard work and will. You have to work towards it step by step because no matter what we try or do, we will always have to work for it in the end. So, it is imperative to work towards your goal and accept the fact that you can't achieve it without patience and dedication.

We have to start by improving ourselves day by day. A slight change a day can help us make a more considerable change for the future. We should feel the need to make ourselves better in every aspect. If we stay the way we are, tomorrow, we will be scared of even a minor change. We feel scared to let go of our comfort zone and laziness. That way, either we or our body can adapt to the changes that make you better, that makes you attract better.

1. **Start With Yourself First**

We all know that every person is responsible for his own life. That is why people try to make everything revolves around them. It's no secret that everyone wants to associate with successful, healthy, and charming people. But, what about ourselves? We should also work on ourselves to become the person others would admire. That is the type of person people love. He can also easily attract positive things to himself. It becomes easier to be content with your desires. We need to get ourselves together and let go of all the things we wouldn't like others doing.

## 2. Have A Clear Idea of Your Wants

Keeping in mind our goal is an easy way to attract it. Keep reminding yourself of all the pending achievements and all the dreams. It helps you work towards it, and it enables you to attract whatever you want. Make sure that you are aware of your intentions and make them count in your lives. You should always make sure to have a crystal-clear idea of your mindset, so you will automatically work towards it. It's the most basic principle to start attracting things to you.

## 3. Satisfaction With Your Achievements

It is hard to stop wanting what you once desired with your heart, but you should always be satisfied with anything you are getting. This way, when you attract more, you become happier. So, it is one of the steps to draw things, be thankful. Be thankful for what you are getting and what you haven't. Every action has a reason for itself. It doesn't mean just to let it be. Work for your goals but also acknowledge the ones already achieved by you in life. That way you will always be happy and satisfied.

### 4. Remove Limitations and Obstacles

We often limit ourselves during work. We have to know that there is no limit to working for what you want when it comes to working for what you want. You remove the obstacles that are climbing their way to your path. It doesn't mean to overdo yourselves, but only to check your capability. That is how much pressure you can handle and how far you can go in one go. If you put your boundaries overwork, you will always do the same amount, thus, never improving further. Push yourself a little more each time you work for the things you want in life.

### 5. Make Your Actions Count

We all know that visualizing whatever you want makes it easier to get. But we still cannot ignore the fact that it will not reach us unless we do some hard work and action. Our actions speak louder than words, and they speak louder than our thoughts. So, we have to make sure that our actions are built of our brain image. That is the way you could attract the things you want in life. Action is an essential rule for attracting anything you want in life.

## 6. Be Optimistic About Yourselves

Positivity is an essential factor when it comes to working towards your goals or dreams. When you learn to be optimistic about almost everything, you will notice that everything will make you satisfied. You will attract positive things and people. Negative vibes will leave you disappointed in yourself and everyone around you. So, you will have to practice positivity. It may not be easy at first while everyone around you is pushing you to negativity. That is where your test begins, and you have to prove yourself to them and yourself. And before you know it, you are attracting things you want.

## Conclusion

Everyone around us wants to attract what they desire, but you have to start with yourself first. You only have to focus on yourself to achieve what you want. And attracting things will come naturally to you. Make sure you work for your dreams and goals with all your dedication and determination. With these few elements, you will be attracting anything you want.

# Chapter 2:

# 9 Tips on How To Have A Strong Relationship

Who doesn't want a strong relationship? Everyone wants to have that high-level understanding with their partner that lasts a lifetime. It is scientifically proven that people who are in healthy relationships have less stress and more happiness.

Healthy relationship not only helps us increase our overall feelings of happiness, but stress-reduction also helps us improve our overall quality of physical and mental health that make every-day life more pleasing to go through. Relationships can be in the form of family, work, friendships, and also romantic ones. Depending on the area that matters the most to you at this very point in your life, you can choose to focus on that specific one until you feel you are ready to focus on the next.

If building powerful relationships is a priority of yours as it is mine, then stay with me till the end of this video because we will be discussing **9 Magical** Tips on How To Have A Strong Relationship with whoever you want. Let's Begin.

**Number one**

**Listen to Each Other**

This is the first and probably the most important thing that you might want to take note of. Just think, how many arguments have you had that went in the wrong direction just because no one was willing to simply just listen? In order to understand each other's point of view both parties must be willing to open up their ears instead of their mouths first. You need to have the stamina to listen to their side of the story before airing yours.

If you truly want a healthy relationship then the foundations starts with a good listening ear. To listen not only when the other party have problems in their lives, but also when they have a problem with you. Develop a good sense of compassion and empathy in the process.

Bitter thoughts, grudge-holding, and negativity toward the other person only serve to weaken your relationships, not strengthen them. So try to understand each other, let the other person speak, and then sort things out in the best possible way.

**Number two**
**Give Time For The Relationship To Grow**

For any relationship to truly blossom, it is important to spend the necessary quality time together. Whether the relationship is with family members, friends, or lovers, it takes energy and effort nonetheless. Any amount of energy you spend on that person will reap its benefits later. Now, I am not saying to drastically change your life or to go on adventures or expensive dates to make your relationship healthy. All you have to do is simply get yourself free for a day or night once a week and do something different together, like having a date night, playing games, cooking and eating, watching movies or whatever you like, just give your best at that time. Be present with them and don't be distracted checking your phone or replying work messages.

## Number three
### Give Time To Yourself

Now I needed to talk about this one right after the number two. I think a good relationship should be balanced. In the previous point, I talked about spending quality time in relationships, but I also don't mean that you should give all your energy to them or stop doing things that energizes your soul. Don't sacrifice your own hobbies for the sake of others. I agree that you need to take more initiative in relationships but at the same time you need to take care of your own happiness too. So give time to yourself and spend it doing things that fills your soul with happiness and gratefulness. You will feel recharged and fresh as a result when you engage in your relationships.

## Number four
### Learn To Appreciate Little Things

This point will touch more on the romantic relationship side of things. If you are in a relationship for quite a while then there is a chance that you might get complacent and too comfortable. You might also gradually forget the little things that make the person special. As a result the other person could potentially feel like you may be taking them for granted. To avoid this, you need to start making it a constant reminder to yourself to appreciate the little things your partner does for you. Say "I love you" to them, give cute little gifts, give them surprises and tell them how much they mean to you. You need to show your partner how much you love them so they never feel taken for granted. So yeah, start doing all this and make your bond strong!!

## Number five
### Learn To Forgive

It is well said, "relationships require a lot of forgiveness". As I mentioned earlier, bitter thoughts and grudge-holding just hurt your relationship in the long run. So if you want a happy relationship then you should learn to forgive. If there is something on your mind that your partner did and you can't forget then sit and talk to them about it and try to come up with a good solution. If any of you makes any mistake, you should forgive them with a smiling face and tell them that these little mistakes can't lessen your love. Work on yourself, make your heart ready for what you see coming and even what you don't see coming, and let things go in the right direction. You need to make your heart learn to forgive, this is the only key.

## Number Six
### Don't expect your partner to complete you

You should be confident about whatever you have. If you are looking for a healthy relationship then you should not expect your partner to complete you. Sometimes, we expect things from our partners which we lack and it can put a strain on your relationship. What you could do instead is to constantly work on yourself to the point that you feel you truly and rightfully deserving of every good thing that comes your way. That you feel secure and independent at the same time in the relationship. Loving yourself first goes a long way in maintaining a strong and healthy relationship with others.

## Number Seven
### Ways Of Showing Love

Different people show and receive love in their own unique ways. Understanding how the other party expresses or receives love is the key to building a strong relationship. Some people do it by caring for you while others express it through physical affection like hugs and kisses. If you don't know that the specific love language is between you and the other party then it might cause problems in the long run. To really ensure the other party feels loved you have to express it in the way that they receive the most strongly. Go find out what they are by asking them and then start giving it right away!

## Number eight
### Be Flexible

If you want a healthy relationship then you have to learn to be flexible as well. Flexible in the face of any changes that might occur in your relationship. It is a known fact that change is the only constant in life. We may never be prepared but we should do our best to adapt to new situations that we may find ourselves in. It is also therefore unrealistic not to expect our relationships to change as time progresses as well. Learn to adapt and grow in this new stage and you will be all the more happier for it.

**Number nine**
**Make Decisions Jointly**

A good and healthy relationship requires listening to each others' desires and concerns. While you may not always love to do the things that the other party wants, you should always try to find a compromise that suits both of your needs. Instead of insisting and making decisions all the time, try making decisions together that both of you will find enjoyable. Be it where to hang out, what to eat for a meal, where to go on a trip together, or even what kinds of products to buy for your home, make sure that the other party's points of view is heard so that they don't end up resenting you over the long run.

**So that's it, guys, we are done with our today's topic of 9 Tips on How To Have A Strong Relationship. Now, it's time for you to share your thoughts. What do you think about these tips? Have you already tried them and do they work? And if you know some other**

tips to make relationships strong then share them in the comment box to help others. If you got value then smash the like button and don't forget to subscribe to our channel as we will be talking about some amazing topics in the future. See you soon!

# Chapter 3:

# <u>7 Ways To Achieve Harmony In Personal Relationships</u>

How beautiful the world or life would be if we were all blessed with harmonious relationships. The kind that is selfless, giving, and nurturing, the kind that doesn't have any tussle of egos and power play. Just you and your significant other fitted together, like a hand in the glove. Harmony isn't an inherent trait; that is one of the reasons why it becomes too difficult for relationships to flow seamlessly. Here are some tips and tricks to build a harmonious relationship with others.

### 1. Harmony Can Be Nurtured

Before getting into the ways to let go of all the negativities and build a holistic, harmonious relationship, we must first understand why harmonious relationships are essential. A harmonious person is defined as someone who is easygoing and has the ability to get along well with others. A harmonious bond is something that two people experience without fighting, clashes, or ego tussles. But most of the time, one of the partners might feel negative emotions, which can affect the quality of the relationship. Feeling discontent in a relationship might have distressing and overwhelming experiences, but that does not in any way means that we should lose all hope.

## 2. Be the best version of yourself:

If you look into your personal relationships to compensate for your loneliness, you are bound to get disappointed sooner or later. It indeed takes two to tango, but building a relationship and making sure it lasts has a lot to do with your state of mind. You have to be peaceful with yourself first before achieving peace in your personal relationships. Over-expecting things from your partners or others would always lead to disappointment, which will, in turn, channel into challenges and difficulties in your relationship. You have to be the bearer of harmony that you wish to cultivate in your relationships. You can start by fixing the broken things on your end, and others will eventually follow you.

## 3. Embrace acceptance:

Resistance and harmony can never go hand in hand. If you wish to achieve harmony, you have to let go of resisting the current order of things or change. Resistance can be in the form of criticizing your partner for whatever behaviors and traits they possess and forcing them to change who they are. This would lead to negativity and tension in the relationship. Going from resistance to acceptance is a passable road that will lead you towards building a harmonious relationship. You have to be aware that no one is perfect, even ourselves. We are bound to make mistakes and have flaws and have to accept others and their defects and errors.

## 4. Let go of the hurt and negativity:

Sometimes, it's our baggage of the past that keeps us unable to build a harmonious relationship. For example, it might be something that your ex-partner did to immensely hurt you, or a family member criticized you. However, you didn't process this hurt nor gave it the time to heal, but instead decided to bottle up your decisions and move on. It is only natural that the negative feelings you are keeping inside you for a long time will come out when someone bad triggers you. In this case, you have to find a way to let go of whatever hurt you're feeling, channel all your negativity, and foster harmony in your relationships.

### 5. Practice compassion:

You have to internalize gentleness and compassion, both as an individual and a couple if you want to build a close and harmonious relationship. When you address and approach any conflict and issue with gentleness, your mind will automatically respond with empathy rather than jumping to conclusions. This will facilitate open communication and inhibitions. It will also enable you to view the other person's perspective and views with kindness. This would put you in a position to give your partner space to process their thoughts and emotions.

### 6. Free yourself from expectations:

The stringent expectations we might feel from our loved ones can take a toll on our equation with them. While it is only natural to expect some things from the people we love, we shouldn't set them in stone. Because unmet expectations lead to a handful of negative emotions of disappointment, hurt, and anger, you end up saying hurtful things to other people. Instead of expecting too much, accept them as they are, allow them to be their own person, and appreciate the good they bring into the relationship. Appreciate their efforts even if they don't go your way.

### 7. Give and seek space in your relationships:

Personal space is one of the rarest yet one of the most crucial elements of feeling at peace in your relationships. Oftentimes, we get so much tethered with our loved ones that it feels like a permanent embrace. It may seem exciting and comforting at first, but soon it will leave you guys feeling suffocated from each other. We must understand that everyone needs their space t catch a breath, reflect, unwind and grow. It is also a hallmark of a healthy bond. To build a harmonious relationship, you must dismantle the clingy approach and give each other all the space you need.

### Conclusion:

A harmonious relationship needs sustained efforts and nurturing, and you can neither expect to achieve harmony overnight nor do expect it to last forever once achieved. But it is sure is worth every effort. The importance of building a harmonious relationship lies in the fact that it brings you peace and hope, the two things most vital to any individual.

# Chapter 4:

# Happy People Surround Themselves with The Right People

Whether we realized it or not, we become like the five people we spend the most time with. We start behaving like them, thinking like them, looking like them. We even make decisions based on what we think they would want us to do.

For example, there are many research findings that prove we are more likely to gain weight if a close friend or a family member becomes overweight. Similarly, we are more likely to engage in an exercise program if we surround ourselves with fit and health-oriented people.

**So, who are the top 5 influencers in your life?** Do they make you feel positive? Do they inspire and motivate you to be the best version of yourself? Do they support and encourage you to achieve your goals? Or, do they tell you that "it can't be done," "it's not possible," "you aren't good enough," "you will most likely fail."

If you feel emotionally drained by the energetic vampires in your life, you may want to detox your life and get rid of the relationships that aren't serving you in a positive way.

The negative people, the naysayers, the Debbie Downers, and the chronic complainers are like a dark cloud over your limitless potential. They hold you back and discourage you from even trying because they're afraid that if you succeed, you'll prove them wrong.

**Have the courage to remove the negative people from your life** and watch how your energy and enthusiasm automatically blossom. Letting go of the relationships that aren't serving us is a critical step if we want to become more positive, fulfilled, and successful.

Detoxing your life from negative influencers will also allow you to become the person you truly want to be. You'll free yourself from constant judgment, negativity, and lack of support.

**Here's what you can do:**

- Stay away from chronic complainers.
- Stop participating in meaningless conversations.
- Share your ideas only with people who are supportive or willing to provide constructive criticism.
- Minimize your interactions with "friends," coworkers, and family members who are negative, discouraging, and bitter.
- Stop watching TV and reading negative posts on social media (yes, mainstream media is a major negative influence in our lives!).

- Surround yourself with positive and successful people (remember, we become like the top 5 people we spend our time with!).
- Find new, like-minded friends, join networking and support groups, or find a positive coach or a mentor.

If you want to make a positive change in your life, remember, the people around you have a critical influence on your energy, growth, and probability of success.

Positive people bring out the best in you and make you feel motivated and happy. They help you when you're in need, encourage you to go after your dreams, and are there to celebrate your successes or support you as you move past your challenges. Pick your top 5 wisely!

# Chapter 5:
# How To Live Authentically

What does being authentic mean? How do I know if the life I'm leading is authentic? Am I happy with the person I've become? Finally, is authenticity overrated? And if you're anything like me, your train of thought maybe similar. It's easy to forget how to be authentic when we play many different roles throughout the day. We're parents, children, friends, employees, teachers, lovers, members of society. But how do we stay true to ourselves when life gets messy, overwhelming, or stressful? By taking small steps and doing little things that make us feel good. No, scratch that. That makes us feel great. Excellent. Ecstatic. Alive. Grateful for who we are and what we have. But also calm, meditative, reflective. I made a shortlist of simple things that have helped me live more authentically and be closer to my genuine self.

## 1. ENJOY THE LITTLE THINGS

I know – this is a cliché, but I can't deny this simple truth. In all honesty, it can take some practice to train your mind to stop blabbering and start noticing the little things. But once it does, you will. Rejoice in the first rays of sunshine on a hazy morning. Feel their warmth on your skin. Smell that first cup of coffee and exhale with a sigh of blissful pleasure as you take that first sip. Hug your pet. Kiss your loved one. Have fresh flowers on your table. Listen to the ocean. Watch the sunset. Let the wind blow through your hair in the spring. Walk on crispy leaves in the fall. Make snow angels in the winter. You know, the little things. Every day, I make conscious efforts to appreciate and remember the special moments and people in my life.

## 2. DON'T JUDGE OR PUNISH YOURSELF FOR YOUR MISTAKES

We often think it's ok to judge ourselves for a mistake we've made either now or in the past. But what's the use? Instead of beating yourself up, see if you can learn something from your failures. So what helps is writing down what each of your mistakes is trying to teach you and how you can avoid repeating it in the future. But please, don't judge yourself. You did the best you could do.

Sometimes, you'll find your true self with life experience and maturity. Other times, it may be hidden under anxiety and depression, feelings of inadequacy, negative self-talk, self-doubt, and fear. And finding it may take some therapy. But the authentic self has no high expectations of themselves or others and takes life lightly. Instead of constantly doing, running, working, thinking – it *just is*. Innocent and vulnerable, but also strong and independent. For me, *authenticity equals freedom*. So tell me – what does authenticity mean to you? How do you find it? Do you have any tips to add to this list? I'd love to hear your thoughts in the comments below.

# Chapter 6:

# 10 Signs Someone Has A Crush On You

Have that inkling suspicion that someone likes you but you're not 100% sure about it?

Many of you will agree that there is a certain level of thrill and adrenaline rush when it comes to crushing on someone. It could also lead to feelings of anxiety and nervousness as well.

I'm sure you've been in a similar situation before – where you had a crush on someone and not know how to express or be yourself around that person. But at the same time secretly hoping he or she knows you're attracted to them so that you may begin a romantic relationship with them.

What if you're on the receiving end of that crush, how do you identify the signs and signals that the person is sending you?

Here are 10 Signs that someone has a crush on you:

**1.There is a distinct difference in their behavior when they are around you.**

It may not be obvious or easily noticeable, but the guy or girl who is secret crushing on you will most likely be nervous when they are around you, or when they engage you in conversation. They might act shy or coy, and maybe even blush when looking at you.

On the flip side, they might also be more enthusiastic in their approach towards you - by expressing cheerfulness because one some level, you make them happy. A person who likes you will pay more attention to the minor details of what you say and what you do. They might also try to make sure you feel great because they want you to feel comfortable and at ease around them as well.

## 2. They might notice you from a distance.

A person who has a crush on you will likely try to peek a gaze at you from a distance. Whether you are at the same workplace, gym, or friendly hangouts with other friends, if you catch them looking at you more than usual, that is a very big sign that is pointing in your favor. They are also likely to spend a longer time gazing at you or giving you some serious eye contact.

In the digital age, distance could also be in the form of internet presence. They might also try to look you up on your social media channels. A good way to tell is if they start liking your posts and commenting on them. That is their way of entering into your life without being too obvious about it.

## 3. They will always find excuses to come close or talk.

You can easily understand whether someone is interested in you or not by their enthusiasm for interacting with you. Whether it is trying to match their timings for going to the coffee break with you or adjusting their dates with their friends to take you out to the movie, they will never leave one opportunity to chance to spend that golden time with you. They might also find the silliest of reason for just starting a conversation with you - like asking whether you will teach them something new or bring them somewhere for a meal.

## 4. Everything you do is appreciated by them.

As a crush, their goal is to make you notice them. To show you that they deserve your attention and time.

If you are going through a bad day, count on your potential crush to talk to you or to make an effort to help you feel better. It is highly likely that your crush will try their best to encourage and make you laugh as well.

They might also laugh at your silliest of jokes. Take it as a form of flattery as it shows that they want to win you over. At the end of the day, as long as it is genuine, it is always better to be around someone who helps you feel good at the end of the day.

## 5. Lets you know they are always available when you need them.

Another sign that your crush likes you is that they will make themselves available to you as and when you might want to talk. They might be quick to reply your messages when you text them, and they will find time for you whenever they can to engage you in conversations that lets them get to know you more. They might also throw in some hints there to show their interest in you.

## 6. Makes excuses to touch you!

If someone has a crush on you, they will definitely express interest by engaging in physical contact with you. Be it just as an excuse to feel the soft sweat shirt you are wearing or turning your wrist to appreciate your watch, watch out for these signs. Physical touch is a sign of flirting, and you need to pay attention to them. If they go one step further by poking you or touching you from the back, it is a sure-fire way to know that your someone likes you.

## 7. Surprise you!

This might not happen with everyone, but there are some people who likes the art of gifting! Especially when they like someone they want to make them feel special, be it bringing them their favorite chocolates and flowers, treating you to a meal, buying you your favorite drink, or getting you something you told them you liked during the last conversation. These are signs that they are paying attention to the little details about you, and that they are trying to express their attraction for you in the form of gift-giving. Friends don't usually buy things for you for no reason at all, so pay attention to this!

## 8. Borrowing things.

This sign may be rare as well but it could happen. It may sound cliché but when we like someone, we want to keep their things close to us. Any items which belong to you will be special to the person who likes you! Borrowing things could be their way of engaging in interaction with you as well, especially if they are very shy to ask you out.

## 9. **They Compliment your appearance and dressing.**

An easy way to know if someone has a crush on you is if they have nice compliments for the clothes you are wearing, for the styling of your hair, or just simply saying you look good today. We say the same when we go on dates to someone we find attractive. We give them compliments to show the other party that we are interested in them. The next time you receive a compliment from someone you suspect has a crush on you, take note of this point.

## 10. **They Ask You Out**

 If your crush likes you, he or she will most likely ask when you are free to go for a meal or to watch a movie together. They might want to take this time to get you to notice them as more than friends. If they engage in any of the previous 9 signs we have discussed, you could potentially be on a date without even knowing it. So watch out for the signs carefully!.

If however, you are emotionally unavailable, it is perfectly okay to let your crush know at any point that you are not ready for a relationship if you see it being a potential cause of issue for your friendship with them.

Ensure that you first confirm that they do indeed have a crush on you before you take any drastic actions to reject them if you are uninterested.

Now that you know what those signs are, you will know how to respond if someone has a crush on you. Do what you will with the information, just do go breaking too many hearts!

# Chapter 7:

# 8 Ways To Gain Self-Confidence

Confidence is not something that can be inherited or learned but is rather a state of mind. Confidence is an attribute that most people would kill to possess. It comes from the feelings of well-being, acceptance of your body and mind (your self-esteem), and belief in your ability, skills, and experience. Positive thinking, knowledge, training, and talking to other people are valuable ways to help improve or boost your confidence levels. Although the definition of self-confidence is different for everyone, the simplest one can be 'to have faith and believe in yourself.'

Here are 8 Ways To Gain More Self-Confidence:

## 1. Look at what you have already achieved:

It's easy to lose confidence when we dwell on our past mistakes and believe that we haven't actually achieved anything yet. It's common to degrade ourselves and not see our achievements as something special. But we should be proud of ourselves even if we do just a single task throughout the day that benefited us or the society in any way. Please make a list of all the things you are proud of, and it can be as small as cleaning your room or as big as getting a good grade or excelling in your job. Keep adding your small or significant achievements every day. Whenever you feel low in confidence, pull out the list and remind yourself how far you have come, how many amazing things you have done, and how far you still have to go.

## 2. Polish the things you're already good at:

We feel confident in the things we know we are good at. Everyone has some kind of strengths, talents, and skills. You just have to recognize what's yours and work towards it to polish it. Some people are naturally good at everything they do. But that doesn't make you any less unique. You have to try to build on those things that you are good at, and they will help you built confidence in your abilities.

## 3. Set goals for yourself daily:

Whether it's cooking for yourself, reading a book, studying for a test, planning to meet a friend, or doing anything job-related, make a to-do list for yourself daily. Plan the steps that you have to take to achieve them. They don't necessarily have to be big goals; you should always aim for small achievements. At the end of the day, tick off all the things you did. This will help you gain confidence in your ability to get things done and give you a sense of self-appreciation and self-worth.

## 4. Talk yourself up:

That tiny voice inside of our heads is the key player in the game of our lives. You'll always be running low on confidence if that voice constantly has negative commentary in your mind telling you that you're not good enough. You should sit somewhere calm and quiet and talk to yourself out of all the negative things. Treat yourself like you would treat a loved one when they tend to feel down. Convince yourself that you can achieve anything, and there's nothing that can stop you. Fill your mind with positive thoughts and act on them.

### 5. Get a hobby:

Find yourself something that really interests you. It can either be photography, baking, writing, reading, anything at all. When you have found yourself something you are passionate about, commit yourself to it and give it a go. Chances are, you will get motivated and build skills more quickly; this will help you gain self-confidence as you would gradually get better at it and feel accomplished. The praises you will get for it will also boost your confidence.

### 6. Face your fears:

The best way to gain confidence is to face your fears head-on. There's no time to apply for a promotion or ask someone out on a date until you feel confident enough. Practice facing your fears even if it means that you will embarrass yourself or mess up. Remind yourself that it's just an experiment. You might learn that making mistakes or being anxious isn't half as bad as you would have thought. It will help you gain confidence each time you move forward, and it will prevent you from taking any risks that will result in negative consequences.

### 7. Surround yourself with positive people:

Observe your friends and the people around you. Do they lift you and accept who you are or bring you down and point out your flaws? A man is known by the company he keeps. Your friends should always positively influence your thoughts and attitude and make you feel better about yourself.

## 8. Learn To Strike A Balance:

Self-confidence is not a static measure. Some days, we might feel more confident than others. We might often feel a lack of confidence due to criticism, failures, lack of knowledge, or low self-esteem. While another time we might feel over-confident. We might come off as arrogant and self-centred to other people, and it can eventually lead to our failure. We should keep a suitable amount of confidence within ourselves.

## Conclusion:

Confidence is primarily the result of how we have been taught and brought up. We usually learn from others how to behave and what to think of ourselves. Confidence is also a result of our experiences and how we learn to react in different situations. Everyone struggles with confidence issues at one time or another, but these quick fixes should enough to boost your confidence. Start with the easier targets, and then work yourself up. I believe in you. Always!

# Chapter 8:

# 7 Ways to Become a Good Partner

**Intro:**

All relationships are unique. Different Experiences, personalities, interests, beliefs and culture tell us about the possibility of hundreds of different types of couples. However, some foundational qualities assure us of a lasting and healthy relationship no matter what kind of two people are involved. Whether you are in a relationship right now or you are single, you know what works for you, and you might be neglecting without even giving it a second thought. So, right now, what you should do is sit back, relax and think about what worked for you and what did not in your past relationships and what was lacking. You can also ask the people around you who are in committed relationships and what worked for them. Although the relationship dynamics of everyone are different, there is always something to learn. We are going to tell you a secret here. For a healthy and long-lasting relationship, you need to work on yourself first. We are going to list down 7 ways in which you can become a good partner.

### 1. Be Secure Within Yourself:

So often in your twenties, you feel like you are ready for a lasting relationship, but around that time, most people have not figured out what their passions are, or they are not confident enough. If you still have not figured out your outlet through which you will contribute to the world, and you are trying to lay the foundation of a new relationship, new home, chances are your relationship will not last long because you will feel restless all the time. However, once you have figured out your sense of being, it brings you a sense of contentment. It will be easier for you to maintain the balance between your work and your relationship. If you are secure with who you are, people's comments or words will not be able to bring you down. That can be difficult for people for various reasons, but you will have a happy relationship once you can do it.

## 2. Be Responsible:

You are going to have good days and bad days. There are going to be days where you will wake up sad and grumpy. After the emotion subsides, you should ask yourself what could be the reason for this. You should always take the responsibility of seeing the truth behind your emotion. Was it your partner's behaviour that made you feel left out or like a third wheel? Tell them. If you feel like your partner is taking advantage of your efforts and are working for this relationship as much as you do, talk to them about this. When you are in a relationship like this, these conversations are not always easy, but you need them to create a stronger bond.

## 3. Be Appreciative:

If you show appreciation for little things, it will strengthen your relationship. It could be as simple as calling them and letting them know when will you be home, making dinner or putting the garbage on the curb. All these little things show that you appreciate their existence in your life and are considerate of their time and feelings.

## 4. Laugh Together:

When you laugh as a couple, you open yourself up to your partner; this allows you to be vulnerable. When you can laugh at yourself and themselves in each other's presence, it will build trust towards each other that they will not judge, humiliate or capitalize but rather enjoy these small moments with you.

## 5. Spend Quality Time Together:

If you treat the relationship in your life as a priority, you will want to spend time together. Of course, there will be times when you will be socializing with others, but that will not give you moments of intimacy or bonding. Instead, you need to take time out to be together. You can have dinner at your favourite restaurant, watch a movie, cook dinner together, go hiking or just simply stay at home and watch Netflix and chill.

## 6. Be Their Number One Fan:

All of us can achieve amazing things in life, but when our loved ones appreciate us, it gives us a confidence boost when the people we love are standing behind us, supporting us as we work towards our goals. So as a partner, you need to understand your partner's dreams and goals and support them as they strive to achieve their goals, in good times and bad. You should let them know that you are always going to stand with them. When you know you have your partner's support, it is the best feeling in the world. But always remember, it is a two-way street.

## 7. Be a Good Listen and Observer:

Suppose you want to be a good partner. In that case, you must understand what annoys them. To do that, you should pay close attention to what they are saying. You need to listen to them and understand what makes them happy, what upsets them, but simultaneously you should be observing how they react in certain situations. What makes them nervous, and what makes them comfortable. You will get to know more about them by observing.

## Conclusion:

We listed how you can be a better partner and make your special feel loved, but you should always remember that a relationship is a two-way street, and they should be putting in the same amount of effort. Make sure that your partner has not become lazy in love, and if you think one of you is getting there, you should have some activities that can bring things back on track, but you and your partner should have a mutual understanding.

# Chapter 9:

# 6 Habits of Strong Couples

Relationships don't always come with guaranteed success. They are always a risk for those who choose to fall in love with each other. People open themselves up to the possibilities of heartbreak and getting hurt whenever things don't go their way. They make so much effort and invest a considerable part of themselves into the relationship in the hopes of not getting emotionally betrayed in the end. Relationships can be stressful and difficult to bear, and the couple's habits can have a powerful impact on the relationship. We can either create positive or negative habits, but once we start practicing them, they will eventually become a part of our unconscious act.

Research says that it takes us 21 days to develop a habit, whether positive or negative. When it comes to having a healthy and happy relationship, certain habits can have a positive and powerful impact. Here are some healthy habits that you need to practice every day to become second nature to you and help you build a stronger connection with your partner.

## 1. Always Show Mutual Respect

Respecting your partner is a crucial ingredient for creating a healthy, happy, and long-lasting connection. It is a habit that is worth developing. Expressing respect towards your partner shows your love, acceptance, and warmth towards them. It shows that you value your partner, no matter the differences. Even if you both have a different outlook on life, you mustn't disrespect your partner or put them down. This goes both ways. If your partner disagrees with you, they should show respect towards you. It's not about both of you not agreeing on a situation, but rather how you handle the issue as a team that makes all the difference in the world.

## 2.   Communicate With Each Other

Communication is perhaps an essential quality of a healthy relationship. But there are instances when we can't communicate appropriately with our partners or come off as emotionally unavailable to them. But healthy and happy couples have this game down. They vocalize their feelings and love for each other and offer compliments and gestures. And instead of sweeping the issues under the rug, they discuss all the bad and negative stuff that bothers them. No matter how awkward or uncomfortable you both might feel, it's always essential to talk about your feelings to move forward and grow.

## 3.   Spending Some Time Apart

As much as it is vital to spend time together with your partner, it's equally important to spend it apart. Being able to be independent and doing your stuff is critical in any relationship. You cannot always depend on your partner for things that you can easily do yourself. Spending too much time together can create unhealthy codependency. Both of them should maintain healthy boundaries and autonomy to ensure a long-lasting relationship.

## 4. Love Languages

Gary Chapman came up with the concept that men and women have five love languages. They can either be words of affirmation, receiving gifts, quality time, acts of service, and physical touch. You and your partner need to know which love language suits you both the best. It will help both of you feel loved and stay connected with each other. Furthermore, you must attend to your partner's love language constantly.

## 5. Appreciate Each Other

We often forget to let our partners know that we appreciate them and don't show them much affection and appreciation. We might have it in our mind, but we fail to express and deliver it to them. But it's always important to show your significant other how much you love and appreciate them and their efforts. This could also be done through words, cards, flowers, acts of kindness, and more.

### 6.  Say Sorry and Mean It

Partners step on each other's toes all the time, whether in big or small ways. It might be a disagreement, argument, or a fight, but recognizing your role in your partner's pain is essential. No matter who is at fault, both of you should aim for an apology that expresses empathy, takes responsibility for your wrongdoings, and shows that you're striving to change your behavior.

### Conclusion

Relationships always require time, patience, and love but also healthy habits. It's easier to fall for someone and promise them the world. But if you want to make your relationship long-lasting, efforts are always required. Sometimes, the proper habits are all we need to make what we have with our partners.

# Chapter 10:

# Six Habits of Self-Love

We can show gratitude to ourselves for our different achievements in many ways. It is something that most people overlook as a waste of time and resources. This is a fallacy. It is high time we develop habits of self-love, to recharge our bodies and minds in preparation for another phase of achievements.

Here are six habits of self-love:

## 1. Treating Yourself

It is showing gratitude to yourself by way of satisfying your deepest desires instead of waiting for someone else to do it for you. Take the personal initiative to go shopping and buy that designer suit or dress you have been wanting so badly. Do not wait for someone else to do it for you while you are capable.

Take that much-needed vacation and a break from work to be with your family. Spend time with the people you love and cherish every moment because, in this fast-moving world, the future is uncertain. Secure your happiness lest you drown in depression. The best person to take care of your interests is yourself.

Who will take you out for swimming or outing to those posh hotels if you do not initiate it? Self-love begins when you realize your worth and do not allow anyone else to bring it down.

## 2. Celebrate Your Victories

Take advantage of every opportunity to celebrate your wins, no matter how small. A habit of self-love is to celebrate your achievements and ignore voices that discourage you. Nothing should muffle you from shouting your victories to the world. The testimony of your victory will encourage a stranger not to give up in his/her quest.

It is neither pride nor boastfulness. It is congratulating yourself for the wins that you rightfully deserve. How else can you love yourself if you do not appreciate yourself for the milestones you have conquered? Do not shy away from thanking yourself, privately or publicly, because no one else best knows your struggles except yourself.


## 3. Accept Yourself

To begin with, accept your social and economic status because you know the battles you have fought. Self-acceptance is an underrated form of self-love. Love yourself and accept your shortcomings. When you learn to accept yourself, other people will in turn accept you. They will learn how to accommodate you in the same manner you learned to live with all your imperfections.

Self-loathing dies when you master self-acceptance and self-love. Self-care keeps off self-rejection. You begin seeing your worth and great potential. It is the enemy within that is responsible for the fall of great empires.

The enemy within is low self-esteem and self-rejection. Accept the things you cannot change and change the things in your ability. Do not be hard on yourself because a journey of a thousand miles begins with a single step.

## 4. Practice Forgiveness

Forgiveness is a strong act. When you forgive those who wrong you, you let go of unnecessary baggage. It is unhealthy to live with a heart full of hate (pun intended). Forgiveness does not mean that you have allowed other people to wrong you repetitively. It means you have outgrown their wrong acts and you no longer allow their inconsiderate acts to affect you. Forgiveness benefits the forgiver more than the forgiven. It heals the heart from any hurt caused. It is the best form of self-care yet difficult at the same time. Forgiveness is a gradual process initiated by the bigger person in any conflict. Practicing self-care is by recognizing the importance of turning a new leaf and staying free from shackles of grudges and bitterness.

Unforgiveness builds bitterness and vengeance. It finally clouds your judgment and you become irrational. Choosing forgiveness is a vote on self-care.

## 5. Choose Your Associates Wisely

Associate with progressive people. Show me your friends and I will tell you the kind of person you are. Your friends have the potential to either build or destroy your appreciation of self-worth. They will trim your excesses and supplement your deficiencies. A cadre of professionals tends to share several traits.

Self-care involves taking care of your mental state and being selective of who you let into your personal space. It supersedes all other interests.

### 6. Engaging In Hobbies

Hobbies are the activities we do during our free time to relax our minds and bond with our friends. When doing these hobbies we are at ease and free from pressures of whatever form. We need to take a break from our daily work routine from time to time and do other social activities.

Hobbies are essential to explore other interests and rejuvenate our psyche and morale. Self-love places your interests and well-being above everything else. There is a thin line between it and selfishness, but it is not the latter.

These six habits of self-love will ensure you have peace and sobriety of mind to make progressive decisions.

# Chapter 11:

# 5 Steps To Using Dating Apps Correctly

There's an old saying that goes like, "You have to kiss a lot of frogs first to find a prince," and these days, it applies to online dating. Does online dating feel like an unsolvable puzzle in your quest for finding 'the one" (or whoever it is that you're looking for)? Then worry no more because you're not alone in this. Online dating is an entirely different ballgame from meeting someone in real life. You have all the information you can get your hands on before meeting them. You may have gone through their short profile or may have exchanged a few words via text or email.

All in all, when you meet someone offline, you may have a lot or very little information about that person ahead of time. As they say, the first impression is the last impression; you have to make sure you apply it both in your online and offline life. Here are some ways to use dating apps correctly.

## 1. Choose Your Photos Wisely

As I've said before, that first impression matters, and nothing can make a better dating profile impression than putting up a great photo. Before setting up your profile, take your time to go through the shots that show off your looks and hint at how your personality is. It would be best if you also kept in mind to post some well establishing shots that your match can use to recognize you when you finally meet them in person. Choose one picture of your close-up face and one more distant snap that shows a complete view of your body. Your features should be visible and don't even think to use an old photo to trick your potential match. We might not be the best judge of our faces, so make sure to ask one or two of your close friends about the pictures you are choosing.

## 2.  Work On Your Bio

A picture may be worth a thousand words, but the bio of your profile is still essential. Even if you are the most charming and loveliest person globally, a blank or a terrible bio will get you nowhere with the people using the apps. Some apps give you enough space to write a complete autobiography, while some limit you to a line or two. No matter what limit or space you get, look deep into yourself and start thinking about your personality and traits that make you different from other people. You should be careful about the areas you should avoid and the ones you should enhance in your profile.

## 3.  Expand Your Expectations

Once you have created a fantastic profile, start looking for partners. Don't be too picky considering the overwhelming number of people using the apps; the possibilities can distract you from the great profiles that are right in front of you. It's normal to find a chance with someone you hadn't considered initially, and it's crucial to venture outside your dating comfort zone. While you should look out for someone with the same opinions and personality as yourself, you shouldn't restrict your options. If you haven't had any luck finding a good match, it may be time to broaden your search terms ad change your criteria. A little flexibility wouldn't do you any harm.

### 4. Remain Active

You may find yourself getting bored after using the apps for an extensive period. However, it is essential to keep your profile up to date, remember to log in regularly, send messages and run searches, even if you aren't looking for love at the moment. Some algorithms determine what appears on your social apps. So, with every action you take on an app or site, it reveals your preferences and allows you to receive more likely matches. Similarly, if you fail to check the app regularly, it will stop sending the appropriate profiles your way.

### 5. Make The First Move

If you potentially get your match and hang out with them, make the first move and ask them out. No matter if it's the guy or the girl, if your intentions are clear about the other person, then it shouldn't stop you both from seeing each other. Ask for their schedule and plan a date whenever they're available. Make them feel comfortable first and get them to trust you so they can go out with you without any hesitation.

### Conclusion

Bring the fun element into dating apps, and don't just make it seem like you're doing some work. Be patient because things like these take time. Keep engaging and stay positive; you might now meet someone instantly.

Explore your options and then hope for the best. If you need to take a break, do it, and then come back when you're ready to dive in again.

# Chapter 12:
# Happy People Engage in Deep Meaningful Conversations

Psychologist Matthias Mehl and his team set out to study happiness and deep talk. In the journal Psychological Science, his study involved college students who wore an electronically activated recorder with a microphone on their shirt collar that captured 30-second snippets of conversation every 12.5 minutes for four days. Effectively, this created a conversational "diary" of their day.

Then researchers went through the conversations and categorized them as either small talk (talk about the weather, a recent TV show, etc.) or more substantive discussion (talk about philosophy, current affairs, etc.). Researchers were careful not to automatically label specific topics a certain way—if the speakers analyzed a TV show's characters and their motivations, this conversation was considered substantive.

The researchers found that about a third of the students' conversations were considered substantive, while a fifth consisted of small talk. Some conversations didn't fit neatly into either category, such as discussions that focused on practical matters like who would take out the trash.

The researchers also studied how happy the participants were, drawing data from life satisfaction reports the students completed and feedback from people in their lives.

The results? Mehl and his team found that the happiest person in the study had twice as many substantive conversations, and only one-third the small talk, as the unhappiest person. Almost every other conversation the happiest person had—about 46 percent of the day's conversations—was substantive.

As for the unhappiest person, only 22 percent of that individual's conversations were substantive, while small talk made up only 10 percent of the happiest person's conversations.

Does small talk equal unhappiness? Score one for Team Introvert because we've known this all along.

## How to Have More Meaningful Conversations

*instead of*

- "How are you?"

- "How was your weekend?"

- "Where did you grow up?"

- "What do you do for a living?"

*Try*

- "What's your story?"

- "What was your favorite part of your weekend?"

- "Tell me something interesting about where you grew up."

- "What drew you to your line of work?"

## Why Is Happiness Linked with Deep Talk?

Further research is still needed because it's not clear whether people make themselves happier by having substantive conversations or whether people who are already happy choose to engage in meaningful talk. However, one thing is evident: Happiness and meaningful interactions go hand-in-hand.

In an interview with the *New York Times*, Mehl discussed the reasons he thinks substantive conversations are linked to happiness. For one, humans are driven to create meaning in their lives, and substantive conversations help us do that, he said. Also, human beings—both introverts and extroverts—are social animals who have a real need to connect with others. Substantive conversation connects, while small talk doesn't.

# Chapter 13:

# 7 Ways To Keep Your Relationship Fresh And Exciting

At the beginning of a relationship, one can feel the excitement and the sparks that come from the newness of a relationship. For example, the butterflies you feel before going on a date can make you feel surprisingly on top of the world. It is the start of a relationship that makes you feel this way. At the beginning of a relationship, everything feels fresh as your partner surprises you and makes you feel special.

But as time goes on, the relationship becomes boring. This can often lead to an end of a relationship; to prevent this, you could always keep your relationship fresh and exciting. Even though now both of you are not the same person you used to be in each other's eyes, but you could still maintain that tingly sensation by trying to be more surprising.

Here are seven ways to keep your relationship fresh and exciting.

### 1. Keep Surprising Each Other

At the start of every relationship, partners often surprise each other with flowers, gifts, or a surprise date. These surprises cause the other partner to feel beloved. Still, people usually stop surprising their partners with such things as time goes on. By continuing to surprise your partner with gifts, flowers, and sweet notes, you keep your relationship fresh. After a while, you learn about the likes and dislikes of your partner. You can easily use that to your advantage by buying them flowers they like or small presents that make them happy. The happiness caused by these small gestures of love can keep the relationship from becoming dull. So don't let the element of surprise die.

### 2. Ask Them Out On A Date

A relationship often begins with a date, and the date makes you feel nervous and excited. Meeting your partner for the first few times can make you want to look the best version of yourself and continue your efforts to look and be the best for your partners. So don't stop the efforts. Ask your partner out on a fancy date to make them happy. Even if you are just ordering food from outside, you could still light up some candles and set the table with a fancy dinner set. This could make your partner feel special, and the freshness of the relationship doesn't die with time.

### 3. Try Something New Together

Always try to do something new, like watching movies you liked as a teenager or eating something you haven't tried before; it awakes the excitement your partner feels throughout the day. Try going ice skating or skateboarding together as a fun activity, taking time from your adult routine, and going hiking and other activities to have fun together simply.

### 4. Speak About Your Feelings Towards Them

Try voicing your thoughts about them. Don't shy away from words and tell them or remind them regularly how much they mean to you or how strongly you feel towards them; simple sentences like "I love you" can profoundly affect your partner. Please don't take your partner for granted but make them feel good about themselves and tell them how important they are in your life. This can make them appreciate your presence, and the relationship will remain fresh.

### 5. Set Life Goals Together

You and your partner can decide on some goals that you can achieve together as a couple. It can be any goal, as a financial goal, or exploring the world together. You could save money for vacations together. During this journey, you can motivate each other but can still have fun. Moreover, when you work as a team, it will also strengthen your bond.

### 6. Turn Off Your Phone

When spending time with each other, try turning off your phone. This will show your partner how important they are to you. Focus on their words and respond actively. Studies show that a relationship can end when you are more focused on social media apps than on your partner.

Using too many social media apps can distance you from your partner; try spending more time with them than using your mobile phone and reestablish your bond with them.

### 7. Greet Each Other With Excitement

When a relationship begins, we often see couples embracing each other with love and passion even when they met just yesterday. Still, as time passes, couples can be seen greeting each other with just a simple hello or a short hug. Greeting your partner with excitement and enthusiasm can make them long to meet you. They would be excited all day long because of the way you greet them. This can ensure that the excitement of the relationship doesn't die. You can greet them with a warm, comforting hug or simply a few exciting words; saying mushy things can also make them feel loved, like "I missed you" when they come back home from work.

By following the above ways, you can keep your partner happy and your relationship fresh and exciting.

# Chapter 14:

# 9 Signs of a Toxic Relationship

Before getting into the video, let's talk about what's a toxic relationship? Dr. Lillian Glass, a California-based psychology expert defines the toxic relationship as "any relationship [between two people who] don't support each other, where there's conflict and one seeks to undermine the other, where there's competition, where there's disrespect and a lack of cohesiveness."

Signs of toxic relationships are all around us. The question is how do we know if we have one? And what are the exact signs of such a relationship? In this video, I'm going to tell you 9 main signs of a toxic relationship. So let's get right into it.

**Main**

1. Unhealthy Communication Patterns

Passive aggressiveness, aggressive or bullying styles of conversations that your partner engages with you could be a clear sign that something isn't right between the two of you. The relationship can turn toxic very quickly when either partner feels guilted into responding in a submissive way to please the other. Furthermore bad communication can also lead to avoiding talking to your partner. Instead of treating you with love and compassion, if your partner has animosity, criticism, sarcasm, and egoism in most of his conversations with you, then it can lead to hatred and thus poison the relationship. We all want a partner who can speak to us with kindness and understanding rather than someone who speaks to us in a threat-like manner.

## 2. Habits or Cycles of Cheating and lying

If you feel that your partner is cheating on you or lying to you, it will damage your trust in your partner and may also harm the relationship. Once trust is lost, it is very difficult to get it back. You may start to trust your partner in days or months, but the possibility always seems fragile. Relationships with distrust can turn good partners into jealous or suspicious people. Sometimes even your partner's unforgettable compromises can't repair trust if it is badly broken. So, if for some reason you can't trust your partner then the relationship is definitely toxic.

## 3. Your Loved Ones Strongly Disapproves of Your Partner

What people close to you think of your partner is one of the most important factors in determining whether the relationship is beneficial or one that could be toxic. So, make sure to pay close attention to what your friends, family, and loved ones are saying about your partner.

Your family and friends always want you to be safe and happy, so if they strongly dislike your partner then there must be a strong reason behind it. They may be able to see red flags in them that you might have otherwise overlooked that may point towards something toxic brewing. That reason or some hateful reactions of your loved ones against your partner can indicate that the relationship is not good for you.

### 4. Over-Dependency On Your Partner

It has been noted by several personality experts that those who are the least self-sufficient (but also most self-critical) tend to be the most toxic partners. Sometimes this is a symptom of an underlying relationship problem. Sometimes it is not. But when a partner is absent-minded or disinterested in "self-care", that can be a red flag.

### 5. Constant Fears of Being Judged

Signs of toxic relationships can also include the feeling like you are constantly being judged. You may wonder why you always feel like you need to be on your best behavior. Or, you may think that you always get in trouble with your partner. Some partners can even pick fights as a way of getting back at their relationship - and then some feel like nothing's ever going right.

### 6. Feeling like you are being taken advantage of

One of the most important signs of toxic relationship behavior is feeling like you're being exploited. You may feel like you're not really treated with care or value. Perhaps you question whether or not you are important enough. You may worry that your partner sees you as someone they can take for granted.

In fact, one of the core dynamics of toxic relationships is that the less valuable you feel, the less valuable your partner will feel. When you have a deep, internal belief that you are not significant, it can lead to behaviors that are meant to hurt you.

### 7. You Are Always Defending Your Partner

One classic sign of toxic relationship behavior is when you find yourself defending your partner against charges of hurting you or you feel guilty and always come first to apologize to your partner but you are not sure why.

When the lines of communication between you and your partner start to break down, you may find yourself defending your partner instead of talking to solve problems. When you and your partner argue, you may also hear your partner say things like "you just need to learn to get along with people," "your problem is with you, not with me" or "you just want to ruin my life." Such behavior is enough to call the relationship toxic.

### 8. All the compromise comes from you

Nobody can manage a good relationship with a partner if they are the only one doing all compromise, work, and love.

A good relationship can only be built with the cooperation of both life partners. However, if you do everything while your partner does nothing and never gives the relationship a better chance to improve, then, of course, the relationship is toxic to you.

### 9.  Your Partner Suffers From Addictions

The use of drugs, especially alcohol or (maybe) cigarettes, has a devastating effect on all relationships and is a major reason for leaving relationships. If your partner is addicted to drugs, and you think you can't solve the problem then make sure to provide him/her medical help.

But if he/she is not ready at all to get rid of drugs and drinks too much alcohol regularly, you should consider the relationship toxic.

## Closing

So that's it. We are done with our today's topic.

Remember that if you feel that you are in a toxic relationship, don't forget to seek help. Consult your friends and family, be open to their opinions and don't be afraid to end the relationship if it indeed turns out to be toxic. Remember that we only have one life to live and we deserve to be with a partner that can care and love us unconditionally in all the right ways.

Now it's your turn to share your thoughts. Do you know about any other signs of a toxic relationship? Let us know in the comments below. If you got value then hit the like and subscribe button.

# Chapter 15:

# *The People You Need in Your Life*

We all have friends, the people that are there for us and would be there no matter what. These people don't necessarily need to be different, and these traits might all be in one person. Friends are valuable. You only really ever come across ones that are real. In modern-day society, it's so hard to find friends that want to be your friends rather than just to use you.

Sometimes the few the better, but you need some friends that would guide you along your path. We all need them, and you quite possibly have these traits too. Your friends need you, and you may not even know it.

### 1. The Mentor

No matter which area or field they are trying to excel in, the common denominator is that they have clarity about life and know exactly what their goals are. These people can impact you tremendously, helps you get into the winners' mindset, infuse self-belief and confidence in you then you, too, can succeed and accomplish your goals. They act as a stepping stone for you to get through your problems. They are happy for your success and would guide you through the troubles and problems while trying to get there.

## 2.  Authentic People

You never feel like you have to make pretense around these people. Life can be challenging enough, so having friends that aren't judging you and are being themselves is very important for your well-being. This type of friend allows you to be vulnerable, express your emotion in healthy ways, and helps bring a smile back to your face when you're down.

They help you also show your true self and how you feel. Rather than showing only a particular side of their personality, they open their whole self to you, allowing you to do the same and feel comfortable around them.

## 3.  Optimists

These people are the kind you need, the ones that will encourage you through tough times. They will be there encouraging you, always seeing the best in the situation. Having the ability to see the best in people and will always have an open mind to situations. Everyone needs optimism in their lives, and these people bring that.

*"Optimism is essential to achievement, and it is also the foundation of courage and true progress."* -*Nicholas M. Butler.*

## 4.  Brutally Honest People

To have a balanced view of yourself and be aware of your blind spots is important for you. Be around people who would provide authentic feedback and not sugarcoat while giving an honest opinion about you.

They will help you be a better version of yourself, rectifying your mistakes, work on your weak spots, and help you grow. These are the people you can hang around to get better, and you will critique yourself but in a good way, helping you find the best version of yourself. Of course, the ones that are just rude should be avoided, and they should still be nice to you but not too nice to the point where they compliment you even when they shouldn't.

# Chapter 16:

# Happy People Savor the Moment

Learning to "savor the moment" in life is a convenient, free, and effective way to increase your happiness and quality of life and reduce stress. Enjoying what you have can help you to appreciate what you've got rather than lamenting what you don't have and creating stress by striving for too much. Being able to savor the moment with loved ones can bring a stronger connection and sense of appreciation, which leads to better quality relationships and all the benefits of social support that they bring. Learn more about these techniques to savor the moment in life.

### 1. Focus on Details

Sometimes as we go through life, we forget to stop and enjoy the little things; indeed, it's possible to go through an entire day either stuck in your ruminations about the past or anxious over the future, never really seizing the moment and noticing the pleasant things that are happening right now (and passing up positive opportunities right and left). As you savor the moment, notice the little things that can make a day special — the smile of a friend, the kindness of a stranger, the beauty of a sunset

### 2. Focus on Sensations

As you're experiencing your day, notice and memorize the details — especially the positive details — of what's happening around you. Create a memory. Notice the sounds you hear, like the sound of children's laughter in the background. Notice the smells, like the scent of a fresh sea breeze. And how did that wind feel on your face? Noticing these types of sensory details helps you live fully in the moment and can help evoke pleasant memories when you hear music, smell aroma, or feel sensations you experience on the days you want to savor.

### 3.  Focus on the Positive

As humans, we're naturally wired to notice the negative events in life more than the positive, as these are what we need to keep track of to maintain our safety: if we're aware of threats around us, we're more able to launch a defense. However, if we actively focus on the positive, we can stress less and enjoy life more from an increasingly optimistic vantage point. To savor the moment, notice what's going right, and appreciate it. This isn't the same as pretending you're happy when you're not; it's more about noticing the things that lead to greater happiness and reduced stress.

### 4.  Express Gratitude

Feeling gratitude goes along with noticing the positive and is an excellent way to savor the moment. Notice all the nice things that people do for you (and thank them whenever possible), or simply notice what you enjoy about people when they're just themselves (and be sure to tell them that, too). Appreciate what goes right in your day as it happens, and write it down in a gratitude journal at night — it's a surprisingly effective way to both raise your level of daily gratitude and build a record of all the things in your life that can make you happy when you're having a bad day.

# Chapter 17:

# 7 Signs That You're Ready To Take Your Relationship To The Next Level

If you're dating someone long enough, chances are you might know them well now and are ready to take your relationship to the next level. You both work out well together through all the ups and downs, connect with each other, and make each other's life wonderful. So whether you're thinking about making your relationship official by introducing them to your family and friends, moving in with them, or even getting engaged, it can both be scary and exciting when you think about making the relationship serious and taking that leap of faith.

While you should definitely consider if your partner is the perfect match for you, you should also do something that makes sure your partner doesn't slip off your hands. It's essential to keep your feelings honest to yourself and your partner because taking that next step would require being more open, vulnerable, and honest. If you feel that you have a healthy relationship, you can't imagine your life without your partner and are in a good place emotionally, then say no more. Here are some signs to convince you that you should up your game!

1. **You both trust each other fully:**

Being able to trust someone entirely isn't as easy as it sounds, especially in times like these and the world we're living in right now. It's more facile to break someone's trust and betray them rather than being an angel and keeping their secrets. The most significant quality one can look for in a partner is how much they value our trust. If you are confident that your partner will always have your back and you can be weak and vulnerable in front of them, maybe you should consider taking the next step. If you have told something to them in confidence and they don't share the information with anyone, and likewise if you do the same, then you both are fortunate. You should never break your partner's trust and expect the same from them.

## 2. You support each other through the good and bad:

Having someone by your side who you know would always support you, no matter what is nothing short of a blessing. Your partner has always comforted and consoled you through the negative phases and cherished and cheered you through the positive ones. Even if they were dealing with their problems, they made sure you were okay first. People like these are very hard to find. Most of the time, we tend to emotionally drain out or become frustrated by being there for people. But with your partner, you are always ready to lend a helping hand and even an ear, listen to all of their problems and shortcomings and support them every step of the way.

## 3. You both apologize to each other when needed:

One of the major signs of a toxic relationship is when your partner doesn't apologize or take accountability, even if they know they are wrong. These relationships tend to have a dead end. You might have noticed that your partner admits when wrong and apologizes, even if not straight away; they do it sooner or later. They try to sort out the arguments and fights calmly and try to listen to your point of views and opinions too, instead of forcing theirs on you. They make sure that you're okay after the fight and may even make small gestures to make you feel that they are guilty and you are more important than any of the arguments you both get into. Similarly, you do the same for them. This is an excellent sign that you should definitely step up your relationship to the next level.

### 4. You give each other space:

You both have a level of freedom and independence both within and outside the relationship. You both aren't on each other's throat and nerves every second. You both have different hobbies and passions that you pursue. You both can meet your friends alone or hang out by yourself, without stressing over if your partner would mind. This is a sign of a healthy relationship when you don't keep buzzing your partner with unlimited calls or texts, ask them about their whereabouts, or cling to them all day. Everyone deserves some free time of their own in which they can be alone and ponder over things.

### 5. You're on the same page with them:

Even if you and your partner don't share the same goals, hobbies, dreams, passions, or even the same views and opinions, you're still on the same page with them about your values and future. For example, both of you have discussed either having children or no children in the future, getting a destination wedding or a simple one, moving out of the city or across the country, or settling in the same spot where you both are right now. Agreeing on the same stuff shows that you both prioritize the same things and are compatible with stepping up your relationship.

### 6. You feel safe with them:

One of the signs that your relationship is ready for the next step is the feeling of comfort and security when you are with them. You can be your utter authentic self with them without fearing that they might judge you or dislike you. You have shown all of your sides to them, the good and the bad, and they still love you regardless. They like your quirks and don't get annoyed or irritated by your behavior. You also have accepted your partner's flaws and imperfections and still look at them the same way.

### 7. Your family and friends love them:

You have introduced them to your family as well as your friends. You were nervous at first as to if they will like them or not. But your partner turned out to be the charmer and swept your family members as well as your close friends off of their feet. They can't help but ask about your partner the minute you visit them and even tease you about taking the next big step with them. They have started to invite your partner on all the occasions and events to spend more time with them and get to know them better. All in all, your family and friends love your partner, and your partner's friends and family do the same to you.

## Conclusion:

Taking the next big step in a relationship could be confusing and stressful, especially when you find yourself confused and unclear. But if you want to keep someone in your life forever, you have to make sure you make all the efforts to keep yourself with them. So if you have found someone worthy of your time and energy, don't let them go. Instead, cling onto them, and make efforts to keep your relationship floating.

# Chapter 18:

# 7 Ways To Live Together In Harmony With Your Partner

A harmonious relationship can make a person's life happy and beautiful, but, unfortunately, not all of us are blessed with a harmonious relationship. It is essential to work on your relationship in order to make it work. Creating a harmonious bond between you and your partner can make your relationship more healthy and stable. The dream relationship of everybody is to feel loved, accepted, and respected but to achieve such a relationship, and you need to first work on yourself. You need to make sure that you are doing your best at making your partner feel loved.

Most people nowadays want to find their soulmates, but even when they see their soulmates, they don't have a peaceful relationship; the lack of harmony causes this.

Here are 7 ways to live together in harmony with your partner.

**1. Accept Your Partners The Way They Are**

The first step to a harmonious relationship is acceptance. It would be best to accept your partners the way they are; distancing them from yourself because of a simple mistake can lead to a toxic relationship. If you choose to love a person and be with them, you need to accept the good and bad in them. As they say that no one is perfect, we all are a work in progress. When you cannot receive your partner the way they are, a harmonious relationship cannot be achieved. It would help if you allowed them to evolve and support them throughout this journey.

## 2. Be Gentle And Compassionate

When you embody gentleness and compassion, your relationship bond deepens, and there is harmony in the relationship. Instead of jumping to conclusions and reacting dramatically, you need to respond with gentleness and understand your partner's feelings.

Compassion brings grace to a person. To achieve a harmonious relationship, you should give your partner grace to work on themselves, understand, and give them space to evolve and mature. It may take time, but it strengthens a relationship.

## 3. Expectations Should Be Released

With expectations comes disappointment. Expectations are the unspoken standards you expected your partner to live up to. When your partner does not live up to your expectations, you might feel upset or disappointed, but how can you have such high expectations from your partner about things that are unspoken. Work on letting go of these ideals that the society and your subconscious mind created about how a relationship should be. Release the attachment to situations turning out a specific way. Brace yourself for different outcomes of different situations. Don't expect too much from your partner because your partner, like you, cannot always live up to your expectation.

## 4. Personal Space In A Relationship

Every human being needs personal space; we often see couples that are always together. It may feel exciting and comforting at first, but everyone needs their personal space to think and function properly. After being with each other with no personal space, one can start feeling suffocated and may behave negatively. It would help if you had time to breathe, to expand, and to look within. To evolve, you need space. Personal space between couples proves that their relationship is healthy and robust.

## 5. Honesty

Honest communication is not just a factor to achieve a harmonious relationship but also to have any relationship at all. Not being truthful can cause conflicts and problems in a relationship. Moreover, being a liar can be a toxic trait that can cause your partner to end the relationship. But before being honest with your partner, you need to be honest with yourself. Know your true self, explore the good and bad in yourself. Don't hide your mistakes from your partner; instead, be honest and apologize to them before it is too late. Honesty is a crucial factor in achieving a harmonious relationship.

## 6. Shun Your Ego

Ego and harmony cannot simply go hand in hand; where ego exists, harmony cannot be established. Often by some people, ego is considered a toxic trait. This is the ego that stops a person from apologizing for his mistakes, which can create tension among the couple. The stubbornness to do things your way is caused by ego and can easily result in unwanted scenarios. These are not the components of a healthy relationship. So to establish a harmonious relationship, you should remove ego and learn to compromise a bit. By removing ego, you allow yourself to be more flexible and understanding.

## 7. Let Go if Unnecessary Emotional Pain

When you keep hurting over old resentments, you convert that pain into toxic feelings that are not good for a relationship. These poisonous feelings can make you make some bad decisions that may result in your partner feeling unsafe around you. This pain can cause you to bury your positives feeling inside. As a result of this, you may feel pessimistic and may exaggerate minor conflicts into something more. A person must let go of this emotional stress and pain. You can let go by going to a therapist or yoga and meditation. Once you have let go of the pain, your heart is now open to a peaceful and harmonious relationship.

To establish a harmonious relationship, you have to accept and understand your partner and work on yourself. Also, work on your radical integrity.

# Chapter 19:

## 8 Ways To Love Yourself First

"Your task is not to seek for love, but merely to seek and find all the barriers within yourself that you have built against it." - Rumi.

Most of us are so busy waiting for someone to come into our lives and love us that we have forgotten about the one person we need to love the most – ourselves. Most psychologists agree that being loved and being able to love is crucial to our happiness. As quoted by Sigmund Freud, "love and work … work and love. That's all there is." It is the mere relationship of us with ourselves that sets the foundation for all other relationships and reveals if we will have a healthy relationship or a toxic one.

Here are some tips on loving yourself first before searching for any kind of love in your life.

### 1. Know That Self-Love Is Beautiful

Don't ever consider self-love as being narcissistic or selfish, and these are two completely different things. Self-love is rather having positive regard for our wellbeing and happiness. When we adopt self-love, we see higher levels of self-esteem within ourselves, are less critical and harsh with ourselves while making mistakes, and can celebrate our positive qualities and accept all our negative ones.

### 2. Always be kind to yourself:

We are humans, and humans are tended to get subjected to hurts, shortcomings, and emotional pain. Even if our family, friends, or even our partners may berate us about our inadequacies, we must learn to accept ourselves with all our imperfections and flaws. We look for acceptance from others and be harsh on ourselves if they tend to be cruel or heartless with us. We should always focus on our many positive qualities, strengths, and abilities, and admirable traits; rather than harsh judgments, comparisons, and self-hatred get to us. Always be gentle with yourself.

### 3.  Be the love you feel within yourself:

You may experience both self-love and self-hatred over time. But it would be best if you always tried to focus on self-love more. Try loving yourself and having positive affirmations. Do a love-kindness meditation or spiritual practices to nourish your soul, and it will help you feel love and compassion toward yourself. Try to be in that place of love throughout your day and infuse this love with whatever interaction you have with others.

### 4.  Give yourself a break:

We don't constantly live in a good phase. No one is perfect, including ourselves. It's okay to not be at the top of your game every day, or be happy all the time, or love yourself always, or live without pain. Excuse your bad days and embrace all your imperfections and mistakes. Accept your negative emotions but don't let them overwhelm you. Don't set high standards for yourself, both emotionally and mentally. Don't judge yourself for whatever you feel, and always embrace your emotions wholeheartedly.

## 5. Embrace yourself:

Are you content to sit all alone because the feelings of anxiety, fear, guilt, or judgment will overwhelm you? Then you have to practice being comfortable in your skin. Go within and seek solace in yourself, practice moments of alone time and observe how you treat yourself. Allow yourself to be mindful of your beliefs, feelings, and thoughts, and embrace solitude. The process of loving yourself starts with understanding your true nature.

## 6. Be grateful:

Rhonda Bryne, the author of The Magic, advises, "When you are grateful for the things you have, no matter how small they may be, you will see those things instantly increase." Look around you and see all the things that you are blessed to have. Practice gratitude daily and be thankful for all the things, no matter how good or bad they are. You will immediately start loving yourself once you realize how much you have to be grateful for.

## 7. Be helpful to those around you:

You open the door for divine love the moment you decide to be kind and compassionate toward others. "I slept and dreamt that life was a joy. I awoke and saw that life was service. I acted, and behold, and service was a joy." - Rabindranath Tagore. The love and positive vibes that you wish upon others and send out to others will always find a way back to you. Your soul tends to rejoice when you are kind, considerate, and compassionate. You have achieved the highest form of self-love when you decide to serve others. By helping others, you will realize that you don't need someone else to feel complete; you are complete. It will help you feel more love and fulfillment in your life.

## 8. Do things you enjoy doing:

If you find yourself stuck in a monotonous loop, try to get some time out for yourself and do the things that you love. There must be a lot of hobbies and passions that you might have put a brake on. Dust them off and start doing them again. Whether it's playing any sport, learning a new skill, reading a new book, writing in on your journal, or simply cooking or baking for yourself, start doing it again. We shouldn't compromise on the things that make us feel alive. Doing the things we enjoy always makes us feel better about ourselves and boost our confidence.

## Conclusion:

Loving yourself is nothing short of a challenge. It is crucial for your emotional health and ability to reach your best potential. But the good news is, we all have it within us to believe in ourselves and live the best life we possibly can. Find what you are passionate about, appreciate yourself, and be grateful for what's in your life. Accept yourself as it is.

# Chapter 20:

## 8 Signs a Girl Likes You

The human mind is considered one of the most complicated organs, and understanding the female mind can be a hell of a task. In 2017, a professor of neurobiology and behaviour, Larry Cahill, Ph.D., issued the differences between a male and a female mind in his research The Journal of neuroscience. He says that although the total brain size of men is more extensive than women, but a woman's hippocampus, critical to learning and memorization, is more significant than a man's and works differently. The two hemispheres of a woman's brain talk to each other more than a man's do.

Women are fascinating, inspiring, and quite complex creatures. And if you're unsure about the signs that a girl might like you, then you're in it for the long run. Mostly, men are expected to make the first move, like approaching a girl, striking up a conversation, or simply asking a girl out on a date. But women play the lead role in deciding whether a man can initiate romantic advances. They initiate the contact by subtly providing cues if the communication is welcome or not.

It's difficult to decipher a woman's behavior, especially if she's giving you mixed signals. But worry not! we're here to help you see the signs clearly of whether a girl likes you or not. So, save yourself some stress, put your decoder ring on, and let's get started.

Here are 8 signs to know if a girl likes you...

### 1. She makes eye contact and holds it.

While a lot of people shies away when making eye contact, if you see a girl holding it for more than a fraction of a second (3-5 seconds max), then there's a strong possibility that she's into you. Research says that when you see something that your brain likes, it releases oxytocin and dopamine into your system. These hormones make you feel incredibly joyous. Notice her eyes the next time she makes eye contact with you; if her pupils dilate, then she's definitely interested in you.

### 2. She laughs at all your jokes (even the lame ones).

When a woman notices a man she's interested in, she would smile, laugh, and giggle more often around him. Even if your jokes are terrible (everyone agrees), but this girl would act as if you're the funniest guy she's ever met. If she counterattacks you with the same humorous and playful banter instead of getting offended, then she's really interested in you. Relationship expert Kate Spring says humor is a sure-fire sign of confidence. And confidence sparks something deep inside women that sets off instant attraction.

### 3. She mirrors your behavior.

A study published in the Personality and Social Psychology Bulletin proved that subtle "behavioral mimicry" indicates that you're attracted to that person. You might notice that she has adopted your slang, the way that you move your hands while making a conversation, or the pace at which you talk. Jane McGonigal, researcher and author of The New York Times bestseller "Reality is Broken", calls mirroring a love detector. She says, "….the more we feel like we really understand somebody, we're really connecting with them, we're really really clicking with them, the more likely we are to mirror what they're doing physically."

### 4. She makes frequent contact with you.

Instigating conversations can be a lot of hard work for a woman since they expect the opposite gender to start the chit-chat. So, if she's constantly engaging in discussions with you, making efforts by replying to you properly, and getting to know you better, she certainly likes you. Relationship expert Dresean Ryan says, "Believe it or not, something as simple as a good morning text can show someone has deep feelings for you."

### 5. She touches you.

One of the most obvious signs that she's into you is when she touches you. It could be a light brush of her hand against yours, slapping your shoulder playfully, or touching your leg or hair. If she's initiating the touch and does not creep out by yours, instead she seems comfortable with you, then it's a great sign of her being interested in you. According to behavior analyst Jack Schafer, "women may lightly touch the arm of the person they are talking to. This light touch is not an invitation to a sexual encounter; it merely indicates that she likes you."

## 6.  She gets nervous around you.

If you're around and she seems to become quiet all of a sudden or starts avoiding you, then know that she's nervous and not uninterested. She might start playing with her hair, rubbing her hands, interlacing her fingers, blink frequently, or compress her lips. If you also notice that her breathing has become ragged and fast when you've entered the room, then that's a lucky sign for you.

## 7.  She's always available for you.

Whether you're in a middle of an existential crisis at 3 in the morning or simply want to go for lunch, you text her, and she's at your door the minute after. Even if she's busy, she'll move things around her schedule just to fit you in. You can easily tell by her body language and her behaviors that she loves spending time with you. She's always there for you whenever you need something, going through a bad phase, or enjoying life.

## 8.  Her friends know about you.

Women tell their friends everything. And by everything, I mean every single thing. So, if she's confident enough to introduce you to her friends, then consider yourself lucky. If they tease her when you're around or start praising her more in front of you, then there's definitely more to the matter. The approval of family and friends is the most critical aspect in seeing whether the individual cares enough to see a future with you.

## Conclusion:

Figuring out if a woman likes you is a very tricky business. You might get silences or mixed signals in the initial few days. But it would be best if you looked for the social cues that women give off when they're attracted to you. Try your best and do not give up, you'll eventually get her!

# Chapter 21:

# Dealing With Worries

Everyone worries from time to time. Too much worry can be bad as it leaves us feeling tense and anxious. Even though we might say to ourselves and others – "Stop worrying. It's pointless. It won't do any good" – there is something about worrying that makes it hard to stop. This is because worry can be helpful.

**Useful worry prompts action. All other worry is pointless.**

• Worry is useful if it makes you pay attention

Worrying about the weather cannot stop it raining on your washing; however, if you watch the sky and act to bring in your washing when it rains, being aware that it will have helped.

• Worry is useful, provided it is turned into a plan for action

For example, worrying that your electricity might get cut off might lead you to act to pay your bill on time. Once the bill has been paid, the worrying would stop, and you would feel better.

• Worry is useful if it helps you be better prepared

Worry may help you think about "what you could do if…," or "what would happen if…". Worrying "what would happen if my house was burgled" could make you act to take out house insurance and lock your front door when you go out.

**Worry without action does nothing**

I worry on its own did something then we could worry all day to increase our bank balance. On the other hand taking action such as selling something, working more hours, or spending less will directly affect our bank balance.

**Is it worth worrying about?**

Four things are not worth worrying about, but that account for many of our worries: the unimportant, the unlikely, the uncertain, and the uncontrollable. Ban these from your life, and you will worry less.

**The Unimportant**

It is easy to fill your life with worries about little things. When you find yourself worrying, start to question yourself instead. Ask yourself, "How important is the thing that I am worried about?"

Here are three points to help you answer this question.

1. **The five-year rule**: Ask yourself: "will this matter in 5 years?" This is a way of looking at your worry from a long-term point of view. View your worries differently: will this still be a concern in a week, a month, or a year?

2. **The measuring rod:** Ask yourself: "Where, on a scale of bad experiences, is the thing I'm worried about?" Think about a very

bad experience you have had. How does your current worry feel when compared with this?

3. **The calculator:** Ask yourself: "How much worry is this worth?" We only have a certain amount of time and energy. Make sure you do not spend more worry on your problem than it is worth. You need your time and energy for more important things. Maybe some time you would have spent worrying could be used for doing something.

# Chapter 22:

## _5 Scientific Tricks To Become Perfectly Happy_

Being happy comes naturally. Almost everything around us makes us happy in a certain way. Being happy is a constant feeling inside a human being. They always tend to get satisfied, even at a minimum. Everywhere we look nowadays, we see things filled with this bright emotion. We tune to the songs written about happiness, we see posters at every corner about being happy, and most importantly, we have people who make us happy. Being happy comes freely, without any fee.

There are scientific ways to become happy because an average human is always looking for more.

Some ways in which you'll feel full at heart and eased at mind. A burst of good laughter is like medicine to the core. So, science has given us ways to take this medicine without and cautions. Being happy is one of the least harmful emotions. It binds people together. Even some forms have been scientifically proven to work in favor of our happiness. There is almost no end to those bright smiles on our lips or those crinkles by our eyes. As it said, smiling is contagious. And we all prefer to smile back at everyone who smiles at us automatically. Here are some scientific ways to be happy.

## 1. Minutes Into Exercise

It is proven that some exercise helps you to smile and laugh more. If there is an exercise to be happy with, then people would be sure to give it a try now and then. Exercise helps us to regulate our jaw muscle, so it will be easier to pass a smile next time. There is also meditation. It enables you to calm your mind and leads towards an easier life. It usually helps to keep you at peace so you'll feel happier towards the things that should make you happy. You'll start to get more content at certain or small items. It becomes a habit slowly to smile more, be more satisfied. Being happy also benefits others, and then they will be more inclined to be pleased towards you.

## 2. Get Enough Sleep

Another scientifically proven way to get happy is to sleep enough every night. It helps with the formation of a proper mindset towards your happiness in life. Sleeping at least 8 hours a day is a must for being happy; if not, the 7 hours would suffice enough for you to smile a little more. It keeps your mind and soul at a steady pace, which is inclined to keep us calm and collected. Keeping calm and organized is one of the factors to be happy. Wake up early to listen to the birds or go for a morning run. Keep yourself fresh in the morning to be a better and happier person.

Early to bed is a wise men choice. So, get a sound slumber every night to have a sunny morning following you.

### 3. Take A Break Now and Then

Even the greatest minds need some rest, so it's only average for a human to get some rest after a long period of working day and night. Go on a vacation. Get a leave because life needs to be enjoyed through anything. Working all the time makes you dull and unhappy. So, make sure to take a break once in a while to start again with a fresh mind and perform a better duty. Don't load yourself with the things that won't matter in a few years. Take vacation so you'll have a more peaceful time ahead of you in your life.

### 4. Build Your Happy Place

People tend to get tired quickly and often by working all the time. All most of the time, vacation can't seem like an option. So, the best place to visit in such a situation is your happy place—a place you have created in your mind where you are so glad all the time. Just by imagining such a place, you get comfortable and tend to keep working and being pleased with the same time. Your happy place gives you joy, and you become a happier person overall. And it is just easier to carry your vacation with you all the time.

## 5. Count Your Achievements

A great way to be scientifically happy is to count all the achievements you have made so far. Even count little things like watering plants as an achievement because it gives you a sense of joy. Achievements tell you that you have done more in your life than you intended to, and you will get motivated to do more every time. It makes you believe in yourself and get you going only forwards. You get happy with the deeds you have done till now, and it helps you plan your next good achievement. You naturally become more inclined to fulfill your desires and needs. All the things you have done so far will make you feel beneficial to society and happier for yourself.

## Conclusion

Being happy is a great feeling with a more remarkable result in life. So, smiling more won't do you any wrong; in fact, it may be good for you to stretch your jaw a little. Happiness doesn't discriminate, so it will be good to spread this scientific happiness as much as we can. Being happy gives us a sense of undeniable joy and a vision of a positive and bright future.

# Chapter 23:

# 7 Habits of Healthy Relationships

Relationships are the social strings that hold us together. We are tied to our loved ones by relationships. Sadly, we also regret being linked, by our relationships, to people of questionable character. There are those relationships we are in by default and others by design – meaning we are in them in our free will, without any coercion whatsoever.

Here are 7 habits of healthy relationships:

1.  <u>Making It Symbiotic</u>

It is a selfish foundation but it is what relationships truly are. Healthy relationships are symbiotic between the partners. Both parties benefit from its existence. They are equal partners and bring something to the table.

When partners in a relationship have a mutual interest in a course, they will work towards achieving it. They understand that any failure is a loss to all of them. This is a powerful drive to make them work towards staying united because they need each other.

Symbiosis is the mechanism of adaptation to nature. The relationship between bees and flowers is an example of a healthy relationship. The bees depend on nectar from flowers to make food while flowers depend on bees to be agents of cross-pollination. It is a win-win for both of them.

## 2.  Pursuing A Common Goal

Two heads are better than one. When people are united by a course they believe in, the relationship is stronger and healthier. There is a reason more than their selfish interests that brings them together.

The promise of success by achieving this common goal makes the relationship healthy – devoid of any backstabbing from either party. As long as partners in a relationship have a common objective, nothing can come between them.

If you have a relationship you want to salvage, find a common ground to stand on. This will give you more reason not to give up on the relationship. Consider the relationship between a man and his fiancé. What is common between them is love and the desire to start a family together. Challenges will come their way but whatever holds them together is greater than what divides them. In the end, love wins.

## 3.  They Are Not Exclusive

Some relationships, especially romantic ones, tend to be exclusive to two people. The two people give themselves to each other completely, withholding nothing. Any foreign person that comes between them is considered hostile and unwanted.

However, healthy relationships are not exclusive. They give room to the third voice of reason which will whisper some advice or rebuke some ills they do. The view of a third eye is golden. It will see what the two of you overlook. The simple, repetitive, toxic habits that bring down relationships will not thrive in yours because you have allowed an experienced eye to be the guardian angel.

This is not to imply that there should be no privacy. Privacy is beautiful in relationships. It only stops being one when it overrides your well-being and stops your relationship from budding.

## 4. It Happens Naturally

Murphy's law states that *anything that can go wrong will go wrong.* Relationships are not exceptional either. Regardless of how many times you try to resuscitate a dying relationship, if it can go wrong then it will go wrong.

Healthy relationships are those that happen automatically. There is no within or external force that works on making them stick. There is a special vibe from those in the relationship. They bond naturally. Partners in automatic relationships do not struggle to be together, it is as if nature herself has blessed them 'to be fruitful and multiply.'

In automatic relationships, you do not ignore the red flags. This kind is not blind. When you see red flags in your relationships and continue living in denial, murphy's law will apply. Settle down to re-evaluate; is it that your spouse is too perfect, or are you ignoring the red alerts all over?

## 5. Balanced Selfishness

What a vice for healthy relationships to thrive in! They are selfish enough to put their interests above those of everyone else. Do not judge; it is completely natural in this world of survival for the fittest. Most importantly is that those in relationships act as a unit. They are not selfish to each other but to the rest of the world.

This vice waters the success of relationships. Not everyone has your best interests at heart. Some will try to infiltrate your relationship and cause havoc. Beware of such people. It is the reason why relationships must be selfish.

Consider the example of bees. They jealously and viciously guard their queen and the honey they make. They are selfish with it and their safety is non-negotiable. Even bee farmers have to wear protective clothing when they want to harvest honey. Their selfishness is what unites them, how beautiful!

### 6. Making Investments

Investment is a sign of trust. You invest in someone or something you have confidence in. Partners in healthy relationships invest in each other because they trust in each other. The best foundation of healthy relationships is trust because in it, you can be yourself.

Why should you be in a relationship with someone you cannot trust? The fact that you cannot be yourself with your partner is sufficient not to be involved with them.

You invest in relationships because you are assured of returns. The safest place to be is in a fulfilling one. Healthy relationships go far because their partners invest their time and resources in them.

### 7. Clearly Marked Boundaries

Regions and territories are demarcated by boundaries. They partition countries, provinces, and estates. So important are they that border disputes are treated with utmost seriousness anywhere in the world. The latest border dispute in East Africa being the unresolved maritime dispute between Kenya and Somalia.

Likewise, healthy relationships have boundaries. The partners are mature enough not to suffocate each other. It is paramount that in a relationship, for example, between a man and his fiancée, that they allow each other space to live their lives.

Healthy relationships are not suffocating or dominating. There is a boundary that those in relationships do not cross. If not for anything else, it is for peace to prevail. It does not mean that trust is lacking in the relationship. On the contrary, it signals that you trust your partner enough not to betray whatever relationship you share.

These 7 habits are paramount for healthy relationships. When you religiously observe them, you will have a testimony of a turning point in your relationships.

# Chapter 24:

# Ten Habits You Must Stop If You Want To Manifest What You Want In Life

We all have our deep secret desires of what we would want to turn into buried in our hearts. We hardly say it aloud lest we are judged harshly by an ungrateful society. It is ungrateful because the same society that celebrates when you in your win shall bash you when you slip.

You may have tried out very many things to bring to life your not-so-alive wishes but your efforts have been in vain. Here are ten things that you must stop if you want to manifest what you want in life:

1. Trusting Everhbody

You may have heard of an old saying that you should keep your friends close and your enemies even closer. This is true especially when you are about to make a major move. Open trust is often violated and you will suffer a series of heartbreaks if you do not cease handing people your trust on a platter.

Trust is earned. Let your friends earn it by continuously proving their loyalty and friendship to you. If you give the wrong people your trust, they will stand in your way of manifesting what you want in life. They will poison your dreams and before you know it, you have lost it all.

2. Sharing yYour Plans Openly

It is not everybody who has your best interest at heart. Some people close to you could be orchestrating your downfall and the more information you reveal the easier it is to bring you down. Be unpredictable if you want to manifest what you want in life.

Manifestation requires some degree of secrecy. Work in silence and let your success introduce you. Stop being an open book for others to read. What could be an innocent act of honesty can turn the tables against you and hinder manifestation.

3. Procrastination

To procrastinate is to postpone action to a later time without proper reason. Sometimes an idea would strike your mind and instead of implementing it immediately, you decide to wait to act after some time. This will make you lose sight of what you wanted to do.

Procrastination kills unborn dreams and is an enemy to your progress. Strike the rod when it is hot. You can consult with people you trust before taking a concrete decision after which you must not delay implementing it.

4. Taking Issues Lightly

There is a big problem when you consider everything at face value. There is always more than what meets the eye. Stop assuming what people say on something concerning you and investigate their motive. This is how you will sift genuine friends from fake ones.

Question the obvious if you have any doubt. This will make you have clarity of mind to make sober decisions. Manifestation requires sobriety. What you overlook or assume could make a great difference in decision-making.

5. Blaming Other People

Great people do not play the blame game. Instead, they innovate solutions to existing problems. They are proactive in society and this makes them stand out in a highly polarized environment.

Stop blaming people for your woes, real or perceived, and work towards not falling into the same trap again. Excuses stand in the way of the manifestation of your dreams. Do not cry foul every time things go wrong. Choose to make them right and chart your way forward. Two wrongs do not make a right.

6. Allowing Other People To Make Deciison On Your Behalf

Why should someone else make decisions for you while you are not incapacitated? They could be biased to your dreams and make key decisions out of line with your goals. Stop giving them the mandate to run your life, do it yourself.

It is right to accept advice and heed it but it does not mean that your advisors should make decisions for you. You choose whether or not to heed the advice. The ultimate responsibility of decision-making rests with you.

7. Casting aspersions On Your Ability

You should not doubt your ability or competence; when you do, nobody will believe you. Self-doubt gives other people the license to demean and underestimate your ability. Manifestation requires self-confidence on your part.

In his book, *the 48 laws of power,* Robert Greene writes that you should enter action with boldness. Conversely, you sign your death warranty when you timidly shy away from challenges thrown your way.

## 8. Disrespecting Authority

Rebellion to authorities is a sign of weakness and bad character. Respect authority from the family to the national level because they are in place to bring equality and level the playing field for its people from all races and backgrounds.

How can you expect manifestation for what you want in life when you are rebellious to the same authority supposed to take care of you? You will similarly be disrespected when you are in a position of power.

## 9. Being Pessimistic

Pessimism has closed potential doors of breakthrough for many people. It crushes any hope of success left. To succeed in what you do, you need to take the initiative despite the odds being against you. You will not see anything good when you are pessimistic.

A pessimistic mind is an enemy of progress. It makes you your own worst enemy. Remove this barrier and start thinking positively and you will make great gains in life.

## 10. Making A Comparison Of Your Life With Others

Life does not come with a manual. Everybody has their question paper to tackle. You therefore cannot copy from anyone else. It is disastrous when you copy the lifestyle of somebody else. You lose your identity when you judge yourself by another person's standards.

Your success is different from your neighbors'. Be encouraged when you clap for other people until your turn arrives. Stop judging yourself harshly if you have not won like your neighbor. Celebrate with them as you count the blessings at your doorstep.

In conclusion, it is agreeable that there are bad habits we ought to stop if we want to manifest what we want in life. These ten habits shed light on a dozen others that we need to stop to achieve manifestation.

# Chapter 25:

# How to Love Yourself First

It's so easy to tell someone "Love yourself" and much more difficult to describe *how* to do it. Learn and practice these six steps to gradually start loving yourself more every day:

**Step 1: Be willing to feel pain and take responsibility for your feelings.**

Step 1 is mindfully following your breath to become present in your body and embrace all of your feelings. It's about moving toward your feelings rather than running away from them with various forms of self-abandonment, such as staying focused in your head, judging yourself, turning to addictions to numb out, etc. All feelings are informational.

**Step 2: Move into the intent to learn.**

Commit to learning about your emotions, even the ones that may be causing you pain, so that you can move into taking loving action.

**Step 3: Learn about your false beliefs.**

Step 3 is a deep and compassionate process of exploration—learning about your beliefs and behavior and what is happening with a person or situation that may be causing your pain. Ask your feeling self, your inner child: "What am I thinking or doing that's causing the painful feelings of anxiety, depression, guilt, shame, jealousy, anger, loneliness, or emptiness?" Allow the answer to come from inside, from your intuition and feelings.

Once you understand what you're thinking or doing that's causing these feelings, ask your ego about the fears and false beliefs leading to the self-abandoning thoughts and actions.

## Step 4: Start a dialogue with your higher self.

It's not as hard to connect with your higher guidance as you may think. The key is to be open to learning about loving yourself. The answers may come immediately or over time. They may come in words or images or dreams. When your heart is open to learning, the answers will come.

## Step 5: Take loving action.

Sometimes people think of "loving myself" as a feeling to be conjured up. A good way to look at loving yourself is by emphasizing the action: "What can I *do* to love myself?" rather than "How can I *feel* love for myself?"

By this point, you've already opened up to your pain, moved into learning, started a dialogue with your feelings, and tapped into your spiritual guidance. Step 5 involves taking one of the loving actions you identified in Step 4. However small they may seem at first, over time, these actions add up.

**Step 6: Evaluate your action and begin again as needed.**

Once you take the loving action, check in to see if your pain, anger, and shame are getting healed. If not, you go back through the steps until you discover the truth and loving actions that bring you peace, joy, and a deep sense of intrinsic worth.

Over time, you will discover that loving yourself improves everything in your life—your relationships, health and well-being, ability to manifest your dreams, and self-esteem. Loving and connecting with yourself is the key to loving and connecting with others and creating loving relationships. Loving yourself is the key to creating a passionate, fulfilled, and joyful life.

# Chapter 26:

# *Five Habits That Can Make Someone Like You*

Favor and love are won. It is an endless race in life that requires zeal. You have to appeal to the other person so that they can like you back and return some affection. We often struggle to make those around us realize that we like them. Sometimes we succeed and at other times, we learn (not lose). The struggle is real and we need to measure up to the task.

Here are five habits that can make someone like you:

### 1. Compliment Them Genuinely

Do not underestimate the power of a simple compliment on someone. A compliment is an indication that you recognize the other person's excellence in something. Appreciate their dressing, skills, effort or assistance lent to you by saying a 'thank you or you look amazing today!' When you make people feel loved by often genuinely complimenting them, they get motivated and feel loved. Always give genuine compliments and avoid faking them because it may come out as envy or jealousy. Instead of building bridges with the other person, you would have unknowingly built a wall.

Wouldn't you like someone who genuinely compliments you? Of course, you would. The glory that fills your heart when you are complimented will draw you to the other person. Genuine compliments are given in private or public. It is hypocritical to wait to be in public before you compliment someone. There is no occasion for acknowledging another. As long as it is in their presence, do not shy away from it.

## 2. Support Their Initiatives

Be in the front line to support the businesses and initiatives of those you want to court their attention. Be in their cheering squad and support their businesses and careers in whatever capacity. To be able to make someone like you, first court their attention, and what better way is there than to show up in those activities that matter to them?

If you develop the habit of being their ambassador in their businesses, they will see that you both have aligned goals and may take a keen interest in you. Their liking for you will grow as you appreciate their work and interests. Supporting their initiatives also means advising them on matters you are competent in. Your input should not be sycophancy but aimed at making a change.

Those you want to like you will do so in appreciation of your invaluable input in their work. Your ties will be stronger and they will like you more beyond your unconditional support. Be careful to maintain the relationship between you two. It is fragile more so that you are the one initiating it and it is up to them to fall for it.

## 3. Stand Up For Them

What can your friends say about you in your absence? This is a rare quality that most people look for when searching for potential friends or associates. If you want someone to like you, stand up for them in their absence. Your testimony about them to other people should be positive, one that will inspire their love for you.

You cannot possibly expect someone to like you if you speak negatively about them behind their back. Your words will haunt you should the one you intended for hears it. It should be something that you can confidently repeat to their face. Your sanctity will make you stand out when you stand up for your friends (pun intended).

Standing up for people you want to like you is a good way of 'shouting' your support for them. They will rush to see who it is that defended their character in public and will develop a special liking for you. Furthermore, you should do this in a manner that attracts respect and decorum to the one you are publicly defending.

## 4. Be Dignified

You are what you attract. It begins with your attributes and how you carry yourself around. This plays a significant role in the perception of other people towards you. What is their opinion about you? Is it desirable enough to make them like you? Work on how you present yourself to other people and you will be irresistibly likable.

There is never a second chance to make a first impression. It is up to you to ensure that the first impression which sticks is the correct one. Carry yourself with dignity in everything you do because you never know who is watching. Random strangers will automatically like you as they observe your personal and public life.

## 5.  Be Humble

Humility is a rare virtue in most people. Nobody wants to be associated with violent friends because their rage makes them unpredictable. Humbleness does not mean you have allowed people to mistreat you. It means you are intelligent enough to choose your battles wisely.

Humble people are likable to a fault. People are attracted to calm personalities. They look mature, responsible, and chaos-free. Portray a positive image of yourself and you will be amazed at how people will like you.

Incorporating these five habits in your routine will make people like you and the icing of the cake is that whoever you aim to like you could be among them.

# Chapter 27:

# Happy People Spend Time Alone

No man is an island except for similarly as we blossom with human contact and connections, so too would we be able to prosper from time burned through alone. Also, this, maybe, turns out to be particularly important right now since we're all in detachment. We've since quite a while ago slandered the individuals who decide to be distant from everyone else, except isolation shouldn't be mistaken for forlornness. Here are two mental reasons why investing energy in isolation makes us more joyful and more satisfied:

## 1. Spending time alone reconnects us.

Our inclination for isolation might be transformative, as indicated by an examination distributed in the British Journal of Psychology in 2016. Utilizing what they call "the Savannah hypothesis of satisfaction," transformative clinicians Satoshi Kanazawa of the London School of Economics and Norman Li of Singapore Management University accept that the single, tracker accumulate way of life of our precursors structure the establishment of what satisfies us in present-day times. The group examined a study of 15,000 individuals matured somewhere between 18 and 28 in the United States. They found that individuals living in more thickly populated regions were fundamentally less cheerful than the individuals who lived in more modest networks.

"The higher the populace thickness of the prompt climate, the less glad" respondents were. The scientists accept this is because we had advanced mentally from when mankind, for the most part, existed on distant, open savannahs. Since quite a while ago, we have instilled an inclination to be content alone, albeit current life generally neutralizes that. Also, as good to beat all, they tracked down that the more clever an individual was, the more they appreciated investing energy alone. Along these lines, isolation makes you more joyful AND is evidence of your smarts. We're in.

## 2. Spending Time Alone Teaches Us Empathy

Investing in a specific measure of energy alone can create more compassion towards others than a milestone concentrate from Harvard. Scientists found that when enormous gatherings of individuals encircle us, it's harder for us to acquire viewpoints and tune into the sensations of others. However, when we venture outside that unique circumstance, the extra headspace implies we can feel for the situation of individuals around us in a more genuine and significant manner. Furthermore, that is uplifting news for others, but different investigations show that compassion and helping other people are significant to prosperity and individual satisfaction.

"At the point when you invest energy with a specific friend network or your colleagues, you foster a 'we versus them' attitude," clarifies psychotherapist and creator Amy Morin. "Investing energy alone assists you with growing more empathy for individuals who may not find a way into your 'inward circle.' "On the off chance that you're not used to isolation, it can feel awkward from the outset," she adds. "However, making that tranquil time for yourself could be critical to turning into the best form of yourself."

# Chapter 28:

# <u>7 Ways Your Behaviors Are Holding You Back</u>

Habits and behaviors are what defines a human being and make you who you are. It is what shapes us and defines our lives while making us move towards our future. However, did you know that there are multiple things that hold you back?

These are the behavior that molds us, defines us, holds us back to be the better person and achieves everything that it takes to be perfect. Well, not that anyone is perfect; however, we all can aspire to be! Isn't it so?

Let us explore and discuss the ways that your behaviors hold you back.

1. Not Accepting Your Faults

We have all been guilty of doing the same. Haven't we? I am so sure that each one of you has at least once committed this sin of shifting the blame to someone else and removing it off your shoulders. We are humans, after all; we are governed by our hearts, more than our minds. This is why we are more inclined to never accepting our faults instead of putting the blame on others.

Irrespective of the circumstance, it is necessary that you accept your fault, realize your weakness, and evaluate what needs to be done in order to never repeat the same. Going forward, you must find a way to turn your weakness into strength.

## 2. Having Self-Doubt

A lot of us are seen killing our dreams due to fear of being rejected. Haven't you already done the same a few times? Well, we all have! Self-doubt is one of the silent killers that can do you more harm than any good. If you constantly find yourself doubting your potential and stuck in a negative situation, you need to know that you are holding yourself back.

You can only look forward and attain a prosperous tomorrow when you stop doubting yourself. Self-doubt can be highly injurious, and this is one big reason why you need to stop holding yourself back and take a giant leap forward, or maybe a baby step! Shall we?

## 3. Procrastinating On Everything

No matter how many times we decide not to keep doing it, we keep doing it! Let's face it, and there are way too many distractions for us to procrastinate and sideline our current goals and duties. Say hello to social media! It distracts you way too many times than it should, especially when you are on the verge of serving your last-minute deadlines!

Hasn't it already got way too annoying? If it has, you must take a deep breath and train your mind. This is one of the behaviors that might hold you back. When you find yourself in such a situation, you must stop procrastinating; instead, do what you are supposed to do. Doing this will help you largely concentrate and uplift productivity.

4. Disrespecting Others

Do you often find yourself engaging in putting others down? If yes, then let me tell you that you are only inviting a lot of ill wrath for yourself. Imagine telling yourself that you are incapable, you are not good enough, and stuffs similar.

Similarly, if you do the same things to others, you are dragging everyone down. This is why you must stop being the harsh person that you are being and put your negativity aside. Disrespecting others or putting others down will only do more harm to you and your mental well-being. Why not focus more on what you can do to uplift others, encourage others and bring in more positivity around yourself!

5. Being In Your Cozy Corner

Not literally, but what we mean is you being in your own comfort zone! We all need our own comfort zones to feel safe and secured! But did you know that this is one such habit that holds you back? Yes, it holds you back from achieving a lot many things that you have only dreamt of. When you stay in your own comfort zone, you will never know what you are capable of.

Hence, unless and until you try your hands on something and step out of your comfort zone, you will never know what you are truly capable of. Did you know that the brawny in the business, such as Bill Gates, Warren Buffet, and many other personalities, have all failed in life, at some point or the other! But what would have happened if they would have feared their failure and stayed in their comfort zone for the rest of their lives?

Remember, with the risk comes to the possibility of achieving a reward. Hence, why hold yourself back and stay in your comfort zone when you can explore, wander and try everything that comes your way to know what you are capable of! Imagine what a great learning experience it will be!

## 6. Waiting For The Right Moment

Do you really think that there is a right moment for everything? If there were, then the law of gravity would not have been discovered, neither would we have received more significant innovations in life. Well, it is up to you to choose a moment and act! Yes, it is as simple as that!

If you keep living your life wandering about the right moment that will control your life and that you have your own sweet time to do everything, you will only lose on your precious time. Instead, we all must be accountable for our actions each day and grab the opportunity to try, create, explore, invent, experiment, and a lot more!

## 7. The Image of Being Perfect

Don't we feel that everyone around us is living their perfect lives? Sorry to burst your bubble, it is not so! Thanks to social media, we are always misguided to believe that others live their fairytales while we are sulking in our own lives! This is when we keep pushing ourselves to live a perfect life, be a perfect person and make everyone around us perfect!

But is it practically possible to do so? In fact, with doing so, we tend to set an unrealistic expectation and tends to harm our mental well being and relationships around us. Life is about swinging in the right direction at times, and sometimes in the opposite! Each of these scenarios brings with it its fruits, which must be graced with positivity.

Hence, let me tell you, there is no need for you to be perfect! Be however you are, but be your best version!

**Conclusion:**

Hence, kill these behaviors that hold you back. Instead, break the barrier and strive for a rewarding tomorrow. Let's try being a little different than we are? What say?

CPSIA information can be obtained
at www.ICGtesting.com
Printed in the USA
LVHW051133120122
708210LV00013B/621